The Story of
Sister Adele
and Our Lady of Champion

Fr. Edward Looney
Illustrated by Ayan Mansoori

The Story of Sister Adele
And Our Lady of Champion
Fr. Edward Looney

Fourth Edition

First edition: 2011
Second edition: 2012
Third edition: 2013
Fourth edition: 2023

ISBN: 979-8-9884033-1-9

Nihil Obstat: Rev. Alfred McBride, O.Praem
Imprimatur: Most Rev. David L. Ricken, DD, JCL

Dedication

To all my teachers of faith, from my grandma Elizabeth to the catechists who prepared me for the sacraments and taught me my prayers and catechism. They lived Our Lady's message, whether they knew it or not.

Over the years, Mary, the Mother of Jesus, has appeared to children throughout the world. Have you heard of Fatima or Lourdes or Guadalupe? These are a few of the more well-known stories of Mary appearing to one person or group of people. We call them apparitions.

When Mary appears, she comes with a special message to encourage us to love God more. In years past, Our Lady has appeared many times in Europe, especially in France. But in 1859, she appeared in the United States to a young Belgian immigrant in a small settlement, then called Robinsonville, in Wisconsin.

My name is Adele Brise, and I was born in Belgium on January 30, 1831. I lived a normal childhood with my parents and two sisters. When I was younger, I had an accident which left me blind in one eye. I never regained sight in it.

When I made my First Holy Communion, a few girls and I made a promise to the Blessed Mother that we would become sisters and work as teachers. A few years later, my family needed me to help at home, so I only went to school until the third grade.

By the time I grew up, my mom and dad had decided that we needed to pack our things and move to America. I did not want to go because I remembered I told Our Lady I would join an order of sisters here in Belgium. I went to my parish priest and asked him what I should do. He told me I should go with my parents and if I was to become a sister it would happen in America.

My mom, dad, two sisters, and a cousin of mine all boarded a ship one day and began a journey of a few months to America. When we arrived, my dad decided to go to Wisconsin. He bought some land where other Belgians had settled, and that's where we began to make a living. I was helping my family with their work and would often travel to the grist mill where they made flour.

I saw something very strange on one of those trips. As I was walking down the wooded trail, between a maple and a hemlock tree, I saw a lady dressed all in white. I stood there, but she didn't talk to me. I did not know what to make of it, so I continued walking to the mill.

That night around the dinner table, I told my family about the mysterious woman. My family thought it could be a soul in purgatory who needed my prayers. Purgatory is the place where souls go before they go to Heaven. Our prayers help them go to heaven sooner.

A few days later, on Sunday, October 9, 1859, I was walking to church, which was 10 miles from my home along that same wooded trail. As I came closer to those same trees, the maple and hemlock, I again saw the same woman. This time I was not alone. One of the neighbors and my sister Isabelle were walking with me. They did not see the lady; only I could see her. I was frightened, but we kept walking to church.

Since this was the second time I saw this woman, I knew I needed to talk with Fr. Verhoef, the priest at the church. After he celebrated Mass, I went to confession and told him about these events. I asked him, "What should I say to this woman?" He told me that I should ask her in God's name who she is and what she wants of me. He gave me his blessing, and I left the church with Isabelle and the neighbor lady.

As we walked, we talked about a lot of things. Approaching that same area where the maple and hemlock trees were, I saw the same woman for the third time, dressed all in white, with a yellow sash around her waist, and a crown of stars around her head. This time, I asked her, "In God's name who are you and what do you want of me?"

The woman talked to me. She said she was the Queen of Heaven who prays for sinners. She told me that I should do the same.

I now knew who the woman was; she was the Mother Jesus—Mary!

She then told me that although I had received Holy Communion that morning, I must do more. Mary asked me to make a general confession and offer my communion for the conversion of sinners.

My friends could hear me talking to the lady, but they could not see her, so they asked me, "Adele, who is it? Why can't we see her as you do?"

I told them to kneel because the Lady said she was the Queen of Heaven. They knelt and, quoting scripture, Our Lady said, "Blessed are they who believe without seeing."

The Blessed Mother asked why I was not working as a teacher, as my friends from Belgium had become sisters and were teaching the children.

I desired very much to please her because by doing so, I would please Jesus.

Crying, I asked her, "What more can I do, dear Lady, for I know so little myself"

She told me to gather the children in this area and teach them about Jesus, showing them how to make the Sign of the Cross, receive Holy Communion, and confess their sins. As Mary was leaving, she told me to not be afraid because she would help me.

Our Lady left to return to Heaven, but she had given me a special mission. She wanted me to pray for everyone that they might know and love Jesus. She also wanted me to go to confession. After preparing myself spiritually, I was to teach the children.

I could not believe Our Lady was asking me to do this because I was handicapped. I was blind in one eye, and I didn't have much schooling. I asked myself, "Why was I chosen for this work?" I don't know the answer to that question, but what I do know is you don't need to be perfect to serve the Lord. Even though I couldn't see in one eye, and I didn't go to school for very long, I could teach the children because I loved God and Our Lady very much.

When my sister and I arrived home, I told the rest of my family about what had happened. They believed me and knew we should build a chapel at the place where Mary appeared.

My father helped build two churches during his life. The first one was too small because so many people were coming to pray there, so others helped him build the second chapel.

While he built the chapels, I was walking around the area teaching the children. I walked about 25 miles each way. I would knock on the door of strangers and ask them if I could teach their children. I told them I would do any household chores in exchange for teaching. That is how important this mission was to me. Many of you probably do not like cleaning your room or feeding the dog, but I was willing to do that in order teach the children and to do what Our Lady had asked.

After doing this for about seven years, I became sick and tired. A priest in the area told me I should find other women who would help me teach. Like those sisters who taught me in Belgium, I started a group of sisters to teach children here in the Belgian settlement. Many women helped me for a few years, but often they would leave to do other things with their life. There were a few who stayed with me until the end.

We eventually built a home for the sisters and a school where children could come and live for the school year. It was called St. Mary's Boarding School. Many children came here. Some were orphans and others from poorer families. We always trusted that God would provide enough money and food so we could continue the work Our Lady asked us to do.

Twelve years after I saw Mary, on October 8, 1871, a fire broke out in Peshtigo, Wisconsin. That city was a small lumber community. There was very little rain that year making fires more common. The wind blew heavily that day like a tornado. It took the fire and carried it from Peshtigo across a large body of water called the Bay of Green Bay. The fire began to burn in the settlement where I lived with the schoolchildren and sisters.

When people saw the fire, they did not know what to think. It was burning everything in sight. The only thing they thought of was to come to the chapel and to pray, asking Our Lady to stop the fire and save them. The schoolchildren and I were already praying in the church when people arrived.

We took a statue of Mary and processed around the property asking Mary's help against the fire. We prayed for many hours and could be heard saying the Hail Mary. Rain came on the morning of October 9th, which was the same day that I saw Mary and spoke with her about my future 12 years earlier. The fire burned everything in sight, but it never touched the land where Mary appeared. All of us were safe! Was this a miracle? People said it was.

After the fire, the sisters and I continued to teach. On July 5, 1896, I knew that my health was not good and that my time here on earth was short. I wanted to talk to my good friend Josie. I told her to be kind to the sick and the old and continue to instruct the children in their religion as I had done. A few hours later, my life on earth was complete. I finished my mission and I handed it on to others.

To this day many people still come to the place where Mary appeared in 1859. They come asking Mary to pray to God that they may be healed from their sickness or that someone in their family would find a job. Many people light candles here, and many stop and visit my gravesite.

The story of my life and the mission I was given continues because people come to this holy place, receive Jesus in the Eucharist, and receive forgiveness of their sins in confession.

The mission includes all of us, even you, your brothers and sisters, and your parents. The message I received was a message to witness my faith and beliefs to others so that they may come to know Jesus more.

Live a life that pleases God, and do not be afraid to tell others about your love for Jesus and Mary. And if you don't mind, tell them about what happened in my life in 1859 and the years that followed.

If you continue to live a life worthy of the Gospel, it is my hope that one day you will see Our Lord and Blessed Lady in Heaven. That is my prayer for you.

The End

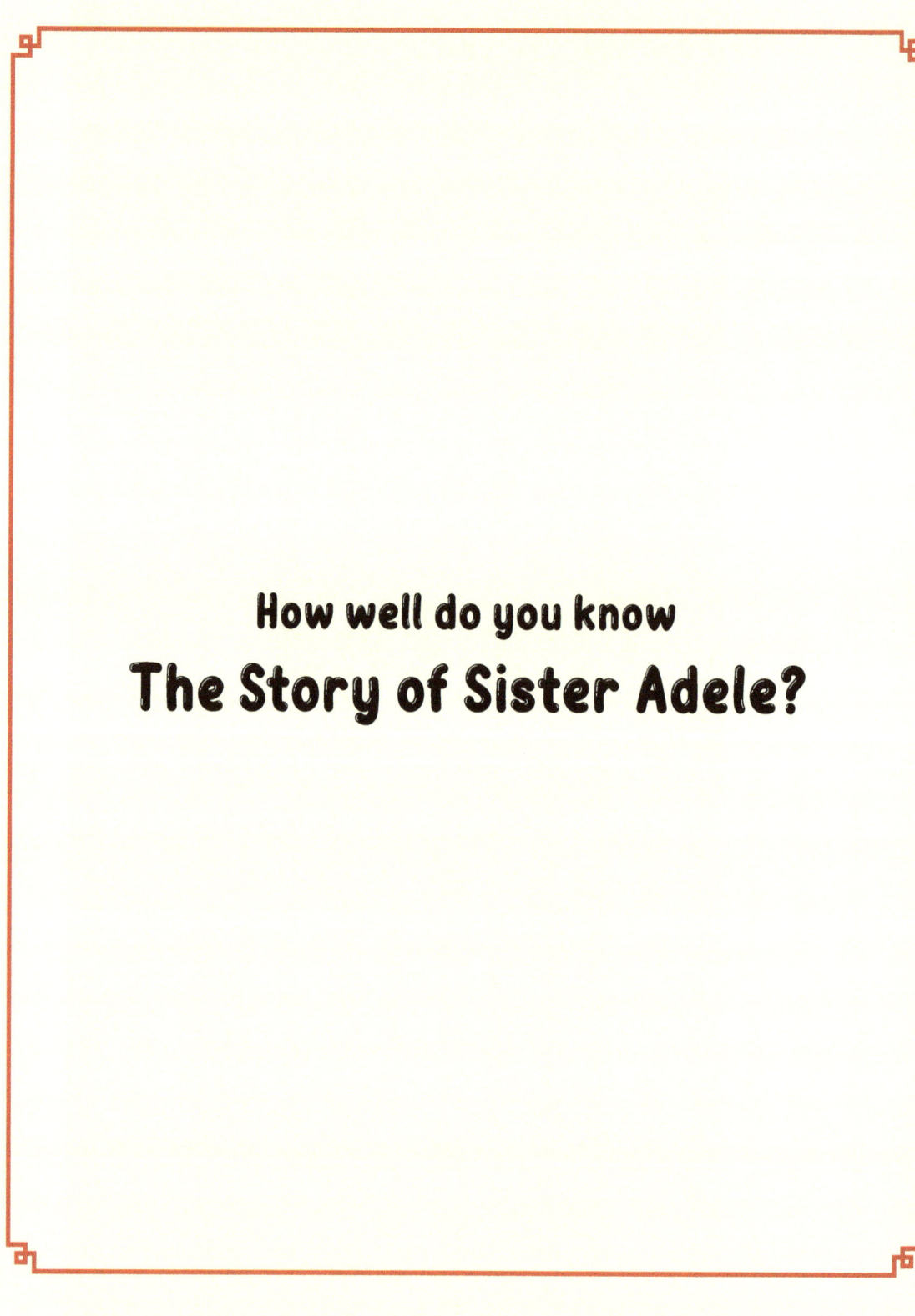

How well do you know

The Story of Sister Adele?

Questions About Mary

1. Where are some places Mary has appeared throughout the world?
2. Why does Mary appear?
3. What do we call these appearances?

Questions about Adele's Childhood

4. Where was Adele born?
5. True or False: Adele was blind in one eye because of a childhood accident.
6. What did Adele promise Mary at her First Holy Communion?
7. Who did Adele talk to before her family left for the United States?

Questions about the Apparition

8. Who did Adele's family think she saw the first time?

9. Who was walking with Adele the morning of October 9, 1859?

10. If Adele saw the woman again, what was she to ask her?

11. Who did the woman in the apparition say she was?

12. What two sacraments did Mary encourage Adele to receive?

13. What more could Adele do?

14. How many times did Adele see Mary?

Questions about Adele's Mission

15.   Who built the chapels where Mary appeared?
16.   How did Adele first teach the children?
17.   What did a priest encourage Adele to do?
18.   What was the name of the school Adele started?

Questions about the Fire

19. Where did the fire begin?
20. What did people do on the night of the fire?
21. What is so important about the date of the fire?

Questions about the Shrine

22. True or False: Sister Adele is buried at the shrine?

23. What are some things people can do when they visit the shrine?

24. How does the mission continue even after Sister Adele's death?

25. What can you do as a young person to fulfil Our Lady's request?

Answers

1. Fatima, Lourdes, and Guadalupe
2. To encourage us to love God more.
3. Apparitions
4. Belgium
5. True
6. Adele promised Mary she would become a sister and teach.
7. The parish priest
8. A poor soul in purgatory
9. Her sister Isabelle and a neighbor lady
10. In God's name who are you and what do you want of me?
11. The Queen of Heaven

12. The Eucharist and Penance (Confession)
13. She was to gather the children and teach them about Jesus, showing them how to make the Sign of the Cross, receive Holy Communion, and confess their sins.
14. Three times; once on the way to the grist mill, on the way to Church on October 9, 1859, and on her return home from church.
15. Adele's father with the help of other people.
16. By walking from home to home, knocking on doors and volunteering to do housework.
17. Adele was encouraged to form a group of religious siters who would teach the children at the school.
18. St Mary's Academy
19. Peshtigo, Wisconsin

20. The people who lived close by went to the chapel and prayed. They carried a statue of Mary around the grounds and prayed the rosary.

21. The fire started on October 8, 1871, the night before the twelfth anniversary of the apparition.

22. True

23. Light candles, pray at Sister Adele's grave, go to Mass, go to Confession, pray the rosary.

24. People still visit the shrine and receive Jesus in the Eucharist and go to Confession. People still are learning the story of Sister Adele and what it means for them.

25. You can witness your faith to other people, live a life that pleases God, and tell others about Mary's apparition to Sister Adele.

About the Author

Fr. Edward Looney was ordained a priest in 2015 and serves as a pastor in the Diocese of Green Bay. He holds a License in Sacred Theology from the University of St. Mary of the Lake and currently serves as the president of the Mariological Society of America. He is an author of popular Marian devotionals for adults including A Heart Like Mary's, A Rosary Litany, A Lenten Journey with Mother Mary and How They Love Mary and for children he has also authored Father Looney's Christmas Stories. His voice is recognizable from his work on EWTN Radio and television and Relevant Radio. He hosts the podcast How They Love Mary and in 2022 completed a 365-day reading of The Mystical City of God by Venerable Maria of Agreda.

www.ingramcontent.com/pod-product-compliance
Lightning Source LLC
Chambersburg PA
CBHW041524120626
46551CB00018B/2567